U0111793

大展好書　好書大展
品嘗好書　冠群可期

大展好書　好書大展

品嘗好書　冠群可期

▲作者的少林拳　Shaolin Boxing of the Author

▲武術雜誌上的耿軍
Geng Jun on the Cover of Wushu Magazine

▲英法武術代表團訪問孟州少林武術院
The Wushu Delegation of France and UK is visiting the Meng zhou Shaolin Wushu Institute

▲作者部分弟子參加武打片拍攝
Parts of students of author take part in fliming Acrobatic fighting film

▲作者與恩師素法大師
The Author and his Teacher Grandmaster Sufa

▲作者指導女兒耿瑞濤練功
The Author is coaching his daughter to practise her skill

▲作者與原國家武術協會主席張耀庭
The Author and the former Chairman of the Chinese Wushu
Association Zhang Yaoting

▲作者的少林拳　Shaolin Boxing of the Author

▲ 武術雜誌封面上的耿軍
Geng Jun on the Cover of Wushu Magazine

▲ 作者與恩師素法大師
The Author and his Teacher Grandmaster Sufa

▲作者率領國外弟子朝拜少林寺　Author leads foreign students to visit Shaolin Temple

▲作者與武僧教頭德揚師兄在捶譜堂
In Chuipu Hall, the author and his senior fellow apprentice
who is also the wushu monk teacher deyang

▲作者與中國政協副主席萬國權
The Author and the vice Chairman of the Chinese People's Political
Consultative Conference （CPPCC） Wan Guoquan

▲作者傳藝國際黑帶功夫總會
The Author is teaching his Wushu skill in International
Black Belt Kungfu Federation

▲作者指導兒子耿鵬飛練功
The Author is coaching his son Geng Pengfei to practise
his skill

少林傳統功夫漢英對照系列　**7**

Shaolin Traditional Kungfu Series Books　

梅 花 拳

Plum-blossom Boxing

耿　軍　著

Written by Geng Jun

大展出版社有限公司

作者簡介

耿軍（法號釋德君），1968 年 11 月出生於河南省孟州市，係少林寺三十一世皈依弟子。中國武術七段、全國十佳武術教練員、中國少林武術研究會副秘書長、焦作市政協十屆常委、濟南軍區特警部隊特邀武功總教練、洛陽師範學院客座教授、英才教育集團董事長。1989 年創辦孟州少林武術院、2001 年創辦英才雙語學校。先後獲得河南省優秀青年新聞人物、全國優秀武術教育家等榮譽稱號。

1983 年拜在少林寺住持素喜法師和著名武僧素法大師門下學藝，成為大師的關門弟子，後經素法大師引薦，又隨螳螂拳一代宗師李占元、金剛力功于憲華等大師學藝。在中國鄭州國際少林武術節、全國武林精英大賽、全國武術演武大會等比賽中 6 次獲得少林武術冠軍；在中華傳統武術精粹大賽中獲得了象徵少林武術最高榮譽的「達摩杯」一座。他主講示範的 36 集《少林傳統功夫》教學片已由人民體育音像出版社出版發行。他曾多次率團出訪海外，在國際武術界享有較高聲譽。

　　他創辦的孟州少林武術院，現已發展成爲豫北地區最大的以學習文化爲主、以武術爲辦學特色的封閉式、寄宿制學校，是中國十大武術教育基地之一。

Brief Introduction to the Author

Geng Jun〔also named Shidejun in Buddhism〕, born in Mengzhou City of Henan Province, November 1968, is a Bud-dhist disciple of the 31st generation, the 7th section of Chinese Wu shu, national "Shijia" Wu shu coach, Vice Secretary General of China Shaolin Wu shu Research Society, standing committee member of 10th Political Consultative Conference of Jiaozuo City, invited General Kungfu Coach of special police of Jinan Military District, visiting professor of Luoyang Normal University, and Board Chairman of Yingcai Education Group. In 1989, he estab-lished Mengzhou Shaolin Wu shu Institute; in 2001, he estab-lished Yingcai Bilingual School · He has been successively awarded honorable titles of "Excellent Youth News Celebrity of Henan Province" "State Excellent Wu shu Educationalist" etc.

In 1983, he learned Wu shu from Suxi Rabbi, the Abbot of Shaolin Temple, and Grandmaster Sufa, a famous Wu shu monk, and became the last disciple of the

Grandmaster. Then recom-mended by Grandmaster Sufa, he learned Wu shu from masters such as Li Zhanyuan, great master of mantis boxing, and Yu Xianhua who specializes in Jingangli gong. He won the Shaolin Wu shu champion for 6 times in China Zhengzhou International Wu shu Festival, National Competition of Wu lin Elites, National Wu shu Performance Conference, etc. and one "Damo Trophy" that symbolizes the highest honor of Shaolin Wu shu in Chinese Traditional Wu shu Succinct Competition. 36 volumes teaching VCD of Shaolin Traditional Wu shu has been published and is-sued by People´s Sports Audio Visual Publishing House. He has led delegations to visit overseas for many times, enjoying high reputation in the martial art circle of the world.

Mengzhou Shaolin Wu shu Institute, established by him, has developed into the largest enclosed type boarding school of Yubei (north of Henan Province) area, which takes knowledge as primary and Wu shu as distinctiveness, also one of China´s top ten Wu shu education bases.

序　言

中華武術源遠流長，門類繁多。

少林武術源自嵩山少林寺，因寺齊名，是我國拳系中著名的流派之一。少林寺自北魏太和十九年建寺以來，已有一千五百多年的歷史。而少林武術也決不是哪一人哪一僧所獨創，它是歷代僧俗歷經漫長的生活歷程，根據生活所需逐步豐富完善而成。

據少林寺志記載許多少林僧人在出家之前就精通武術或慕少林之名而來或迫於生計或看破紅塵等諸多原因削髮爲僧投奔少林，少林寺歷來倡武，並經常派武僧下山，雲遊四方尋師學藝。還請武林高手到寺，如宋朝的福居禪師曾邀集十八家武林名家到寺切磋技藝，推動了少林武術的發展，使少林武術得諸家之長。

本書作者自幼習武，師承素喜、素法和螳螂拳李占元等多位名家，當年如饑似渴在少林寺研習功夫，曾多次在國內外大賽中獲獎。創辦的孟州少林武術院亦是全國著名的武術院校之一，他示範主講的 36 集《少林傳統功夫》教學 VCD 已由人民體育音像出版社發行。

本套叢書的三十多個少林傳統套路和實戰技法是少

林武術的主要內容，部分還是作者獨到心得，很值得一讀，該書還採用漢英文對照，使外國愛好者無語言障礙，爲少林武術走向世界做出了自己的貢獻，亦是可喜可賀之事。

張耀庭題
甲申秋月

Preface

Chinese Wushu is originated from ancient time and has a long history, it has various styles.

Shaolin Wushu named from the Shaolin Temple of Songshan Mountain, it is one of the famous styles in the Chinese boxing genre. Shaolin temple has more than 1500 years of history since its establishment in the 19th year of North Wei Taihe Dynasty. No one genre of Shaolin Wushu is created solely by any person or monk, but completed gradually by Buddhist monks and common people from generation to generation through long–lasting living course according to the requirements of life. As recording of Record of Shaolin Temple, many Shaolin Buddhist monks had already got a mastery of Wushu before they became a Buddhist monk, they came to Shaolin for tonsure to be a Buddhist monk due to many reasons such as admiring for the name of Shaolin, or by force of life or seeing through thevanity of life. The Shaolin Temple always promotes Wushu and frequently appoints Wushu Buddhist monks to go down the mountain to roam around for searching masters and learning Wushu from them. It also invites

梅
花
拳

Wushu experts to come to the temple, such as Buddhist monk Fuju of Song Dynasty, it once invited Wushu famous exports of 18 schools to come to the temple to make skill interchange, which promoted the development of Shaolin Wushu and made it absorb advantages of all other schools.

The author learned from many famous exports such as Suxi, Sufa and Li Zhanyuan of Mantis Boxing, he studied Chinese boxing eagerly in Shaolin Temple, and got lots of awards both at home and abroad, he also set up the Mengzhou Shaolin Wushu Institute, which is one of the most famous Wushu institutes around China. He makes demonstration and teaching in the 36 volumes teaching VCD of Shaolin Traditional Wushu, which have been published by Peoples sports Audio Visual publishing house.

There are more than 30 traditional Shaolin routines and practical techniques in this series of books, which are the main content of Shaolin Wushu, and part of which is the original things learned by the author, it is worthy of reading. The series books adopt Chinese and English versions, make foreign fans have no language barrier, and make contribution to Shaolin Wushu going to the world, which is delighting and congratulating thing.

Titled by Zhang Yaoting

目　錄
Contents

梅
花
拳

說　明

　　（一）為了表述清楚，以圖像和文字對動作作了分解說明，練習時應力求連貫銜接。

　　（二）在文字說明中，除特別說明外，不論先寫或後寫身體的某一部分，各運動部位都要求協調活動、連貫銜接，切勿先後割裂。

　　（三）動作方向轉變以人體為準，標明前後左右。

　　（四）圖上的線條是表明這一動作到下一動作經過的線路及部位。左手、左腳及左轉均為虛線（┄┄►）；右手、右腳及右轉均為實線（——►）。

Instructions

(i) In order to explain clearly figures and words are used to describe the actions in multi steps. Try to keep coherent when exercising.

(ii) In the word instruction, unless special instruction, each action part of the body shall act harmoniously and join coherently no matter it is written first or last, please do not separate the actions.

(iii) The action direction shall be turned taking body as standard, which is marked with front, back, left or right.

(iv) The line in the figure shows the route and position from this action to the next action. The left hand, left foot and turn left are all showed in broken line (┅┅►) ; the right hand, right foot and turn right are all showed in real line (──►) .

基本步型與基本手型
Basic stances and Basic hand forms

圖 1

圖 2

圖 3

圖 4

圖 5

圖 6

梅花拳

圖 7

圖 8

圖 9

圖 10

圖 11

圖 12

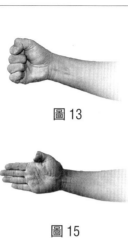

圖 13

圖 14

圖 15

圖 16

圖 17

圖 18

圖 19

圖 20

圖 21

基本步型與基本手型

基本步型

少林武術中常見的步型有：弓步、馬步、仆步、虛步、歇步、坐盤步、丁步、併步、七星步、跪步、高虛步、翹腳步12種。

弓步：俗稱弓箭步。兩腿前後站立，兩腳相距本人腳長的4～5倍；前腿屈至大腿接近水平，腳尖微內扣不超過5°；後腿伸膝挺直，腳掌內扣45°。（圖1）

馬步：俗稱騎馬步。兩腳開立，相距本人腳長的3～3.5倍，兩腳尖朝前；屈膝下蹲大腿接近水平，膝蓋與兩腳尖上下成一條線。（圖2）

仆步：俗稱單叉，一腿屈膝全蹲，大腿貼緊小腿，膝微外展，另一腿直伸平仆接近地面，腳掌扣緊與小腿成90°夾角。（圖3）

虛步：又稱寒雞步。兩腳前後站立，前後相距本人腳長的2倍；重心移至後腿，後腿屈膝下蹲至大腿接近水平，腳掌外擺45°；前腿腳尖點地，兩膝相距10公分。（圖4）

歇步：兩腿左右交叉，靠近全蹲；前腳全腳掌著地，腳尖外展，後腳腳前掌著地，臀部微坐於後腿小腿上。（圖5）

坐盤步：在歇步的形狀下，坐於地上，後腿的大小腿外側和腳背均著地。（圖6）

　　丁步：兩腿併立，屈膝下蹲，大腿接近水平，一腳尖點地靠近另一腳內側腳窩處。（圖7）

　　併步：兩腿併立，屈膝下蹲，大腿接近水平。（圖8）

　　七星步：七星步是少林七星拳和大洪拳中獨有的步型。一腳內側腳窩內扣於另一腳腳尖，兩腿屈膝下蹲，接近水平。（圖9）

　　跪步：又稱小蹬山步。兩腳前後站立，相距本人腳長的2.5倍，前腿屈膝下蹲，後腿下跪，接近地面，後腳腳跟離地。（圖10）

　　高虛步：又稱高點步。兩腳前後站立，重心後移，後腿腳尖外擺45°，前腿腳尖點地，兩腳尖相距一腳距離。（圖11）

　　翹腳步：在七星螳螂拳中又稱七星步，兩腿前後站立，相距本人腳長的1.5倍，後腳尖外擺45°，屈膝下蹲，前腿直伸，腳跟著地，腳尖微內扣。（圖12）

基本手型

　　少林武術中常見的手型有拳、掌、鉤3種。

　　拳：

　　分為平拳和透心拳。

　　平拳：平拳是武術中較普遍的一種拳型，又稱方拳。四指屈向手心握緊，拇指橫屈扣緊食指。（圖

13）

透心拳：此拳主要用於打擊心窩處，故名。四指併攏捲握，中指突出拳面，拇指扣緊抵壓中指梢節處。（圖14）

掌 ：

分為柳葉掌、八字掌、虎爪掌、鷹爪掌、鉗指掌。

柳葉掌：四指併立，拇指內扣。（圖15）

八字掌：四指併立，拇指張開。（圖16）

虎爪掌：五指分開，彎曲如鉤，形同虎爪。（圖17）

鷹爪掌：又稱鎖喉手，拇指內扣，小指和無名指彎曲扣於掌心處，食指和中指分開內扣。（圖18）

鉗指掌：五指分開，掌心內含。（圖19）

鉤 ：

分為鉤手和螳螂鉤。

鉤手：屈腕，五指自然內合，指尖相攏。此鉤使用較廣，武術中提到的鉤均為此鉤。（圖20）

螳螂鉤：又稱螳螂爪，屈腕成腕部上凸，無名指、小指屈指內握，食指、中指內扣，拇指梢端按貼於食指中節。（圖21）

Basic stances

基本步型與基本手型

Usual stances in Shaolin Wushu are: bow stance, horse stance, crouch stance, empty stance, rest stance, cross – legged sitting, T – stance, feet – together stance, seven – star stance, kneel stance, high empty stance, and toes – raising stance, these twelve kinds.

Bow stance: commonly named bow – and – arrow stance. Two feet stand in tandem, the distance between two feet is about four or five times of length of one's foot; the front leg bends to the extent of the thigh nearly horizontal with toes slightly turned inward by less than 5°; the back leg stretches straight with the sole turned inward by 45°. (Figure 1)

Horse stance: commonly named riding step. two feet stand apart, the distance between two feet is 3~3.5 times of length of one's foot, with tiptoes turned forward; bend knees to squat downward, with thighs nearly horizontal, knees and two tiptoes in line. (Figure 2)

Crouch stance: commonly named single split. Bend the knee of one leg and squat entirely with thigh very close to lower leg and knee outspread slightly; straighten the other leg and crouch horizontally close to floor, keep the sole turned inward and forming an included angle of 90° with lower leg. (Figure 3)

Empty stance: also named cold – chicken stance. Two feet stand in tandem, the distance between two feet is 2 times of

梅
花
拳

length of one´s foot; transfer the barycenter to back leg, bend the knee of the back leg and squat downward to the extent of the thigh nearly horizontal, with the sole turned outward by 45°; keep the tiptoe of front leg on the ground, with distance between two knees of 10cm. (Figure 4)

Rest stance: cross the two legs at left and right, keep them close and entirely squat; keep the whole sole of the front foot on the ground with tiptoes turned outward, the front sole of the back foot on the ground, and buttocks slightly seated on the lower leg of the back leg. (Figure 5)

Cross – legged sitting: in the posture of rest stance, sit on the ground, with the outer sides of the thigh and lower leg of the back leg and instep on the ground. (Figure 6)

T – stance: two legs stand with feet together, bend knees and squat to the extent of the thighs nearly horizontal, with one tiptoe on the ground and close to inner side of the fossa of the other foot. (Figure 7)

Feet – together stance: two legs stand with feet together, bend knees and squat to the extent of the thigh nearly horizontal. (Figure 8)

Seven – star stance: Seven – star step is a unique step form in Shaolin Seven – star Boxing and Major Flood Boxing. Keep the inner side of the fossa of one foot turned inward onto tiptoe of the other foot, bend two knees and squat nearly horizontal. (Figure 9)

Kneel stance: also named small mountaineering stance. Two feet stand in tandem, the distance between two feet is 2.5

times of length of one´s foot, bend knee of the front leg and squat, kneel the back leg close to the floor, with the heel of back foot off the floor. (Figure 10)

High empty stance: also named high point stance. Two feet stand in tandem. Transfer the barycenter backward, turn the tiptoe of the back leg outward by 45°, with tiptoe of front leg on the ground, and the distance between two tiptoes is length of one foot. (Figure 11)

Toes –raising stance: also named seven –star stance in Seven –star Mantis Boxing. Two legs stand in tandem, and the distance between two legs is 1.5 times of length of one´s foot. Keep the tiptoe of back leg turned outward by 45°, bend knees and squat, straighten the front leg with heel on the ground and tiptoe turned inward slightly. (Figure 12)

Basic hand forms

Usual hand forms in Shaolin Wushu are: fist, palm and hook, these three kinds.

Fist: classified into straight fist and heart–penetrating fist.

Flat fist: a rather common fist form in Wushu, also named square fist. Hold the four fingers tightly toward the palm, and horizontally bend the thumb to button up the fore finger. (Figure 13)

Heart –penetrating fist: mainly used for striking the heart part. Put four fingers together and coil –hold them, the middle finger thrusts out the striking surface of the fist, the thumb

buttons up and presses the end and joint of the middle finger. (Figure 14)

Palm: classified into willow leaf palm, splay palm, tiger's claw palm, eagle's claw palm, fingers clamping palm.

Willow leaf palm: palm with four fingers up and thumb turned inward. (Figure 15)

Eight–shape palm: palm with four fingers up and thumb splay. (Figure 16)

Tiger's claw palm: palm with five fingers apart, bent as hook and like tiger's claw. (Figure 17)

Eagle's claw palm: also named throat locking hand, with the thumb turned inward, the little finger and middle finger turned onto palm, fore finger and middle finger apart and turned inward. (Figure 18)

Fingers clamp palm: palm with five fingers apart and palm drawn in. (Figure 19)

Hook: classified into hook hand and mantis hook.

Hook hand: bend the wrist, five fingers drawn in naturally with fingertips together. This hook is used in wide range, the hook mentioned in Wushu refers to this. (Figure 20)

Mantis hook: also named mantis' claw, bend wrist into wrist bulge upward, the ring finger and little finger bend to hold inward, with fore finger and fore middle finger turned inward and end of thumb pressed on the middle joint of the fore finger. (Figure 21)

梅花拳套路簡介

Brief Introduction to the Routine Plum-blossom Boxing

　　梅花拳是少林傳統優秀套路之一。本套路動作舒展大方，結構完整，風格獨特。演練起來前沖後打、左騰右落；動作高低起伏，變化多端；招法連貫。因套路似梅花狀，故名梅花拳，適合有一定武術基礎者演練。

　　Plum -blossom boxing is one of excellent routines of traditional Shaolin Wushu. Actions of this routine are decent, with integral structure and distinctive style. When performed or practiced, thrust in the front and strike at the back, jump from the left and fall to the right; the actions heave and set, being most changeful, and postures are interlinked. Because this routine looks like the shape of plum blossom, thus it is named plum - blossom Boxing, which is suitable for the persons who has certain wushu base to perform or practise.

梅花拳套路動作名稱
Action Names of Routine
Plum-blossom Boxing

第一段　Section One

1. 預備勢　Prearatory posture
2. 金雕展翅　Golden roc spreads wings
3. 掛耳捶　Ear-hanging hammer
4. 馬步沖拳　Thrust fist in horse stance
5. 童子拜佛　The boy worships Buddha
6. 猛虎出洞　Fierce tiger goes out of the cave
7. 虛步束身　Shrink the body in empty stance
8. 燕子鑽林　The swallow flies into the forest
9. 踢腿打捶　Kick and punch
10. 獨立打虎　Beat tiger on single leg

第二段　Section Two

11. 翻身劈山　Turn body to chop hill
12. 摟手弓步沖拳　Brush hand and thrust fist in bow stance
13. 彈腿沖拳　Snap kick and thrust fist
14. 弓步沖拳　Thrust fist in bow stance

15. 馬步架打　Parry and punch in horse stance
16. 騰空擺蓮　Jumping lotus kick
17. 小虎抱頭　Little tiger holds the head
18. 猛虎跳澗　Fierce tiger jumps over gully
19. 摟手弓步沖拳　Brush hand and thrust fist in bow
　　　　　　　　　stance
20. 劈腿　Leg split
21. 童子拜佛　The boy worships Buddha
22. 提桶插　Barrel-lifting inserting
23. 大鵬亮爪　The roc spreads claws

第三段　Section Three

24. 海底炮　Cannon at the bottom of the sea
25. 馬步架打　Parry and punch in horse stance
26. 轉身穿喉掌　Turn body to thread throat
27. 後掃腿　Sweeping leg backward
28. 連三掌　Linked three palms
29. 旋風腳　Whirlwind kick
30. 回頭望月　Turn back to look at the moon
31. 二起腳　Jumping kick twice
32. 白鶴亮翅　White crane spreads wings
33. 猿猴束身　The monkey shrinks body
34. 虎尾腳　Tiger-tail foot
35. 猛虎出洞　Fierce tiger goes out of cave

第四段　Section Four

36. 墊步拐肘　Elbow bending with skip step

37. 轉身反背拳　Backhad fist with body turn

38. 撤步打三拳　Step back and punch three times

39. 馬步單鞭　Single whip in horse stance

40. 臥地炮　Ground cannon

41. 沖天炮　Sky cannon

42. 臥枕　Rest on the pillow

43. 地蹚掃腿　Sweep leg on the ground

44. 丁步亮掌　Flash palm in T-stance

45. 猛虎跳澗　Fierce tiger jumps over gully

46. 馬步沖拳　Thrust fist in horse stance

47. 舞花坐山　Swing arms with horse stance

48. 收勢　Closing form

梅花拳套路動作圖解

Action Illustrtion of Routine Plum-blossom Boxing

圖 1

第一段　Section one

1. 預備勢　Preparatory posture

(1)兩腳站立。兩手自然下垂，成立正勢；目視前方。（圖 1）

(1) Stand with feet together, and the hands drop na-turally, keep standing at attention. Eyes look forward.（Figure 1）

圖 2

(2)上動不停。左腳向左橫跨一步，與肩同寬；兩掌變拳，抱於腰間；目視左方。（圖 2）

要點：挺胸塌腰，頭正頸直。抱拳和擺頭快捷。開步輕靈流暢，並同時完成。

(2) Keep the above action. the left foot strides a step left-ward, shoulder-width apart. Change the two palms into fists and hold them on the waist. Eyes look leftward.〔Figure 2〕

Key points: keep chest out and waist lowered, the head upright and neck straight. Hold the fists and turn the head quickly, put apart the two feet lightly and fluently, which shall be completed simultaneously.

圖 3

2. 金雕展翅　Golden roc spreads wings

(1)接上勢。右手在外，左手在內，在腹前直臂交叉；目視雙手。（圖 3）

(1) Follow the above posture, cross the two hands in front of the abdomen with arms straight, keep the right hand outside and the left one inside. Eyes look at the two hands. ﹙Figure 3﹚

圖 4

(2) 上動不停。右腳向前上步,雙手經胸前向上、向外畫弧後向兩側分開;雙臂與肩呈水平,掌心向外,掌指向上;目視前方。(圖 4)

要點:兩個畫弧動作要輕靈迅捷,連貫協調。

(2) Keep the above action, the right foot steps forward, swing the two hands up outward to draw a circle through the front of the chest and then separate them to both sides of the body. Keep the two arms at shoulders level with the palms outward and the fingers up. Eyes look forward. ﹝Figure 4﹞

Key points: the two actions of drawing circle shall be light, quick and agile, consistent and harmony.

圖 5

3. 掛耳捶　Ear‑hanging hammer

⑴接上勢。雙手從兩側下落，右手在外，左手在內；目視雙手。（圖 5）

⑴ Follow the above posture, two hands drop from the two sides of the body, with the right hand outward and the left one inside. Eyes look at the two hands.（Figure 5）

圖 6

　　(2) 上動不停。左腳上步，腳尖點地成高虛步；兩掌經腹前交叉，繼續向上，向外畫弧分掌，兩臂呈水平；目視左方。（圖 6）

　　(2) Keep the above action, the left foot steps forward with toes on ground into high empty stance, cross the two palms through the front of the abdomen, continue to draw a circle upward and outward and separate the palms, keep the two arms horizontal. Eyes look leftward.（Figure 6）

圖 7

(3)上動不停。右腳經左腳前向左上步成插步；同時，兩手變拳，右拳抱於右胸前，左拳收於腰間；目視右方。（圖 7）

要點：抱拳與擺頭動作連貫協調完成。

(3) Keep the above action, the right foot steps leftward throught the front of the left one into back cross step, at the same time, change the two hands into fists, hold the right fist in front of the right chest and draw the left one on the waist. Eyes look rightward.（Figure 7）

Key points: holding the fist, shall be coherent, consistent and harmony with turning the head.

圖 8

4. 馬步沖拳
Thrust fist in horse stance

接上勢。左腳上步成馬步；右拳收於腰間，左拳經右臂內側向左沖拳，拳心向下，與肩同平；目平視左方。（圖8）

要點：上步與沖拳要連貫協調。

Follow the above posture, the left foot steps forward into horse stance, draw back the right fist and hold it on the waist, strike the left fist leftward through the inner side of the right arm, keep the fist −center down at shoulders height. Eyes look leftward. (Figure 8)

Key points: stepping forward and striking the fist shall be coherent and harmony.

圖 9

5. 童子拜佛
The boy worships Buddha

接上勢。身體右轉 90°，兩拳變掌在胸前畫弧，然
後隨著身體上提，在頭頂向兩側分開；上左腳，下蹲
成歇步；同時，兩掌交叉立掌於胸前，右掌在外，左
掌在內；目視前方。（圖 9）

要點：兩掌畫弧與分開要快捷有力，連貫協調。

Follow the above posture, turn the body 90° to the right, change the two fists into palms and draw a circle in front of the chest, and then raise them with the body, separate to both sides of the body on the head top, the left foot steps forward, squat into rest stance, at the same time, cross the two palms and stand them in front of the chest, keep the right palm outside and the left one inside. Eyes look forward. (Figure 9)

Key points: drawing a circle of the two palms and detaching the palms shall be quick and forceful, coherent and harmony.

圖 10

6. 猛虎出洞
Fierce tiger goes out of the cave

（1）接上勢。右腳震腳，身體右轉 90°，併步下蹲；雙手向外環抱於腰間；目視左方。（圖 10）

(1) Follow the above posture, stamp the right foot, turn the body to 90° to the right, put the feet together and squat; the two hands encircle the waist outward. Eyes look leftward.（Figure 10）

圖 11

(2) 上動不停。上左腳成左弓步；雙拳同時向左前方沖出，左拳與肩同高，右拳高過頭頂，拳心相對；上體向左前方傾；目視左前方。（圖 11）

要點：沖拳要抖肩發力，力達拳面；發音以氣催聲，鼻音發出，聲音沉悶。

(2) Keep the above action, the left foot steps forward into left bow stance, the two fists simultaneously punch left forward, keep the left fist at shoulders height and the right fist higher than the head top with the palm sides opposite. The upper body slants left forward. Eyes look left forward.〔Figure 11〕

Key points: when punching the fists, snap the shoulders to exert strength, and the strength shall reach the fist – face: send out nasal sound through breath, and the sound shall be toneless.

圖 12

7. 虛步束身
Shrink the body in empty stance

（1）接上勢。身體右轉 90°成右弓步；雙拳變掌，
向裏、向外翻腕再向前平擺，掌心向下，掌指向前，
與肩同平；目視前方。（圖 12）

（1）Follow the above posture, turn the body 90° to the right
into right bow stance, change the two fists into palms and turn
over the wrist in ward and outward, horizontally swing them
forward, keep the palm down and the fingers forward, at
shoulders height. Eyes look forward. （Figure 12）

圖 13

(2) 上動不停。雙掌向裏、向外翻腕變拳抱於胸前；同時，撤右腳成右虛步；身體後坐；目視右拳。（圖 13）

(2) Keep the above action, turn over the wrists inward and outward to change the two palms into fists and hold the fists in front of the chest. At the same time, withdraw the right foot into right empty stance, the body slants slightly backward. Eyes look at the right fist. 〔 Figure 13 〕

圖 14

8. 燕子鑽林
The swallow flies into the forest

(1) 起身上右腳；雙拳自然向後擺動，拳心向前。
（圖 14）

(1) Raise the body, the right foot steps forward, the two fists swing backward naturally with the fist–palm forward.〔Figure 14〕

圖 15

　　(2) 接上勢。抬左腳、右腳蹬地騰空向前跳步，落地成右仆步。（圖 15）

　　(2) Follow the above posture, raise the left foot with the right one pressing against the guound to jump forward, land to the ground into right crouch stance.（Figure 15）

圖 15 附圖

同時，雙手胸前合抱，左掌附於右拳面；目視右前方（圖 15 附圖）

At the same time, the two hands hold together in the front of the chest, with the left palm pressing on the fist–plane of right fist. Eyes look right forward.（Attached figure 15）

圖 16

(3) 上動不停。重心前移成弓步；右肘向前頂出，
與肩同平；目視前方。（圖 16）

要點：頂肘要抖肩發力，力達肘尖，跳步要快速
敏捷。

(3) Keep the above action, transfer the center forw–ard into
bow stance, thrust the right elbow forward at shoulders height.
Eyes look forward.（Figure 16）

Key points: when thrusting the elbow, shake the shoulders
to apply force, and the force shall reach the elbow joint, jump
forward quickly and agilely.

圖 17

9. 踢腿打捶 Kick and punch

(1)接上勢。起身，右手抱於腰間，拳心向上，左掌附於右掌上面；左腳提起，向前、向上彈踢；目視前方。（圖 17）

(1) Follow the above posture, raise the body, hold the right hand on the waist, keep the fist–palm up with the left palm pressing on the right one. Lift the left foot and kick up forward. Eyes look forward. (Figure 17)

圖 18

(2) 上動不停。落左腳成左弓步；左手摟抓收於腰間；同時，右拳呈水平前沖；目視前方。（圖 18）

要點：沖拳要抖肩發力，快捷迅猛。

(2) Keep the above action, the left foot lands into left bow stance, grab with the left hand, draw it back and hold on the waist, at the same time, horizontally thrust the right fist forward. Eyes look forward. (Figure 18)

Key points: when thrusting the fist, snap the shoulders to apply force, which shall be quick and swift.

圖 19

10. 獨立打虎　Beat tiger on single leg

(1)接上勢。右腳上步併步，震腳，身體略下蹲；左拳擺架於頭頂上方，右拳後擺；目視右拳。（圖19）

(1) Follow the above posture, the right foot steps for—ward, bring the feet together, stamp with the right foot, slightly squat the body downward. The left fist swings and parries above the right part of the head top, the right fist swings backward. Eyes look at the right fist.（Figure 19）

圖 20

　　(2) 上動不停。起身，左腳屈膝上提成右獨立勢；左拳下栽於左膝上，右拳擺架於頭頂右上方，拳心斜向上；目視前方。（圖 20）

　　要點：栽拳與左膝上下協調一致，勁力要合。

　　(2) Keep the above action, raise the body, bend the left knee and raise the left foot into left stance on one leg, the left fist punches downward to the left knee, the right fist swings and parries above the right part of the head top with the fist-palm up aslant. Eyes look forward.（Figure 20）

　　Key points: fist punching down and the left knee going up and down shall be harmonious and consistent, with resultant force.

圖 21

第二段 Section Two

11. 翻身劈山 Turn body to chop hill

(1) 接上勢。向前落左腳，身向右略轉；右拳從上向後、向下、向前繞弧；目視右拳。（圖 21）

(1) Follow the above posture, the left foot lands forward , the body turns to the right slightly. The right fist circles from up to back, down and front to draw a curve. Eyes look at the right fist. （Figure 21）

梅花拳

圖 22

(2) 上動不停。向前抬右腳，左腳蹬地跳起，身體右轉 180°；同時，左手向左上方擺動，右手繼續在身體右側畫一立圓，屈臂護於頭右側；目視左前方。（圖 22）

(2) Keep the above action, raise the right foot for-ward, the left foot presses against the ground to jump up, the body turns 180° to the right, at the same time, the left hand swings left upward, the right hand continues to hold for vertical circle at the right side of the body, bend the arm and put it at the right side of the head for protection. Eyes look left forward.（Figure 22）

圖 23

(3)上動不停。兩腳落地成左仆步；右掌向前下劈掌，左掌收於右腋窩下；目視右掌。（圖 23、圖 23 附圖）。

圖 23 附圖

(3) Keep the above action, the feet land to the ground into left crouch stance, the right palm chops forward and downward, draw back the left palm under the right armpit, Eyes look at the right palm. ﹙Figure 23, Attached figure 23﹚

圖 24

12. 摟手弓步沖拳
Brush hand and thrust fist in bow stance

接上勢。起身，左轉 90°成左弓步；左手前摟變拳收於腰間，右拳向前沖出，拳心向下，與肩同高；目視右拳。（圖 24）

要點：沖拳要帶臂發力，力達拳面。

Follow the above posture, raise the body, turn the body 90° to the left into left bow stance. The left hand grabs forward, changes into fist and draws back to the waist, the right fist punches forward with the fist–palm down at the shoulder height. Eyes look at the right fist. (Figure 24)

Key points: thrusting the fist shall transport force with arm, and the force shall reach the fist–plane.

圖 25

13. 彈腿沖拳
Snap kick and thrust fist

接上勢。沖擊左拳,彈踢右腳,右拳隨即抱於腰
間;目視前方。(圖 25)

要點:彈腿要繃直腳面,與沖拳同時完成,力達
腳尖和拳面。

Follow the above posture, thrust the left fist, kick the with
right foot, then hold the right fist on the waist. Eyes look
forward. ﹝Figure 25﹞

Key points: snap kick shall stretch straight the instep and be
completed simultaneously with thrusting the fist, and the force
shall reach the tiptoe and the fist-plane.

圖 26

14. 弓步沖拳
Thrust fist in bow stance

接上勢。右腳向後落步成左弓步；右拳前沖，拳
心向下，拳眼向左，與肩同高；左拳抱回腰間；目視
前方。（圖 26）

要點：後撤右腳與前沖右拳要快捷有力，協調完
成。

Follow the above posture, the right foot lands backward into
left bow stance, the right fist punches forward with the fist–palm
down and fist–hole leftward at the shoulders height; the left fist
draws back and holds on the waist. Eyes look forward. (Figure
26)

Key points: the right foot stepping backward and the right
fist striking forward shall be rapid and forceful, completed
harmoniously in step.

圖 27

15. 馬步架打
Parry and punch in horse stance

（1）接上勢。右腳向前上一步，身體左轉 90°成馬步；左拳上架於頭頂左上方，右拳向右方沖出，拳心向下；目視右方。（圖 27）

（1）Follow the above posture, the right foot takes a step forward, the body turns 90° to the left into horse stance, the left fist parries left upward above the head top, the right fist punches rightward with fist–palm down. Eyes look rightward.（Figure 27）

圖 28

(2) 上動不停。左腳向右上一大步，身體右轉 180°
成馬步；右拳擺架於頭部右上方，左拳向前沖出；拳
心向下，與肩同高；目視左方。（圖 28）

　　要點：兩個馬步架打動作要連貫協調，一氣呵
成。

(2) Keep the above action, the left foot takes a stride
rightward, the body turns 180° to the right into horse stance; the
right fist parries right upward above the head, the left fist strikes
forward with the fist-palm down at the shoulders height. Eyes
look leftward. (Figure 28)

　　Key points: two actions in horse stance shall be coherent
and harmonious at a heat.

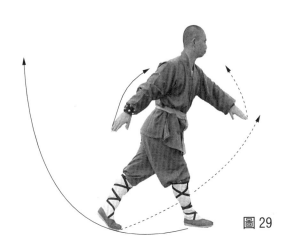

圖 29

16. 騰空擺蓮 Jumping lotus kick

(1)接上勢。起身，身體右轉 90°，上右步，腳尖外展；雙拳變掌，左掌向前，右掌向後擺動；上體前傾；目視前方。（圖 29）

(1) Follow the above posture, raise the body and turn 90° to the right and the right foot steps forward with the tiptoe turning outward, change two fists into palms with the left palm swinging forward and the right one swinging backward, the upper body slants forward. Eyes look forward. (Figure 29)

圖 30

(2) 上動不停。左腳離地，右腳蹬地騰空，在空中外擺；雙手拍擊腳面；目視前方。（圖 30）

(2) Keep the above action, the left foot leaves the ground, the right foot presses against the ground to jump up and swings outward in the air, two hands slap the instep. Eyes look forward. 〔Figure 30〕

圖 31

(3)上動不停。左右腳依次落地分開站立；兩臂向左右兩側呈水平分開，手心向下；目視右方。（圖31）

要點：擺蓮要明顯，拍擊力點要準確響亮。

(3) Keep the above action, the left foot and the right one land to the ground in sequence and stand apart: separate two arms horizontally toward left and right sides with palm down. Eyes look rightward.〔Figure 31〕

Key points: lotus swinging shall be obvious with accurate points of force and loudsound.

圖 32

17. 小虎抱頭　Little tiger holds the head

接上勢。收左腳，腳尖點地下蹲成左丁步；左臂盤肘於腹前，左拳心向下，拳面頂於小腹右側；右拳直劈，經胸前環繞一周後，屈肘擺架於頭頂右上方，拳心向前；目視左前方。（圖 32）

Follow the above posture, draw back bend with toes on ground, and squat into left T-stance, the left arm the left foot elbow in front of the abdomen with the left fist -center downward, the fist-plane presses on the right side of the lower abdomen, the right fist circles with the arm straight through the front of the chest, then bend the elbow and parry with the right fist above the right part of the head top with the fist -palm forward, Eyes look left forward.（Figure 32）

圖 33

18. 猛虎跳澗
Fierce tiger jumps over gully

(1) 接上勢。向左上步，起身；雙掌在頭上方合擊；目視左前方。（圖 33）

(1) Follow the above posture, step leftward, raise the body, the two palms jointly strike above the top of the head. Eyes look left forward.〔Figure 33〕

圖 34

(2) 上動不停。雙腳蹬地起跳，向前躍步；雙掌從上向右摟抱，右掌變拳抱於右腰間，左掌立於右胸前。（圖 34）

(2) Keep the above action, two feet presses against the ground to jump for a step forward, two palms grab from up to right, the right palm changes and holds on the right waist, and the left one stands in front of the right chest.（Figure 34）

梅花拳套路動作圖解

圖 35

(3)上動不停。兩腳落地成左仆步；左掌向左腳上方切掌；同時，身體前傾；右掌變拳，仍抱於右腰間；目視左腳尖。（圖 35）

(3) Keep the above action, the two feet land to the ground into left crouch stance, the left palm cuts above the left foot. At the same time, the body slants forward, the right palm changes into fist and holds on the right waist. Eyes look at the left tiptoe. 〔Figure 35〕

圖 36

19. 摟手弓步沖拳
Brush hand and thrust fist in bow stance

接上勢。起身成左弓步；左手外摟變拳收於腰間；右拳向前沖出，高與肩平，拳心向下；目視前方。（圖 36）

要點：沖拳要抖肩發力，力達拳面。

Follow the above posture, raise the body into left bow stance, the left hand brushes outward, changes into fist and draws back on the waist, the right fist punches forward at the shoulders level with fist −palm down. Eyes look forward. (Figure 36)

Key points: when thrusting the fist, shake the shoulders to release force that shall reach the fist−plane.

圖 37

20. 劈腿　Leg split

(1) 接上勢。起身，雙腿直立；臂屈肘上抬至右肩上方，拳心向裏；目平視前方。（圖37）

(1) Follow the above posture, raise the body, and make two legs stand upright, bend the right elbow and raise the arm above the right shoulder with fist -palm of the fist inward. Eyes horizontally look forward.（Figure 37）

梅
花
拳

圖 38

(2) 上動不停。右腳從下向上、向前踢前額；右拳
同時直臂下劈，左拳仍抱於腰間；目視前方。（圖
38）

要點：右腳前踢要順肩發力，力達腳尖，輕靈快
捷。

(2) Keep the above action, the right foot kicks toward the
forehead from down to up and forward. At the same time, the
right fist chops downward with the arm straight. Keep the left
fist on the waist. Eyes look forward.（Figure 38）

Key points: when the right foot kicking forward, release
force along the shoulder, with the force reaching tiptoe and the
action light and rapid.

圖 39

21. 童子拜佛　The boy worships buddlha

（1）接上勢。右腳落地，身體左轉 90°；雙手變掌在胸前交叉，向左右兩側分掌，掌心向外，掌指向上；目視前方。（圖 39）

（1）Follow the above posture, the right foot lands to the ground, the body turens 90° to the left, change the two fists into palms and cross them in front of the chest, separate the palms leftward and rightward with palm outward and fingers up. Eyes look forward. （Figure 39）

梅花拳

圖 40

(2) 上動不停。收左腳再向前落步成左虛步；兩手在胸前交叉立掌，右掌在外，左掌在內；身體後坐；目平視前方。（圖 40）

　　要點：上下動作要緊密配合，連貫協調。

(2) Keep the above action, draw back the left foot and fall ahead into left empty stance, cross the two hands in front of the chest with palms standing, keep the right palm outside and left one inside, the body slants backward. Eyes look forward horizontally.〔Figure 40〕

　　Key points: the actions shall be concerted closely, coherent and harmonious.

圖 41

22. 提桶插　Barrel-lifting inserting

(1)接上勢。起身右轉 90°，倒插左步；左手向下、向外畫弧，屈臂上提變拳，拳心向裡；右手向外、向下畫弧，直臂於體前，掌心向外；目視右手。（圖 41）

(1) Follow the above posture, raise the bldy, turn the body 90° to the right, and change into left back cross stance; the left hand draws a curve downward and outward, bend and raise the arm and change it into fist with fist-palm inward, the right hand draws a curve outward and downward in front of the body with the arm straight and palm outward. Eyes look at the right hand （Figure 41）

圖 42

（2）上動不停。右腳向右開出一步成馬步；同時，右手變拳，上提於右胸前，拳心向裡，左拳下栽；目視右方。（圖 42、圖 42 附圖）。

要點：栽拳要抖肩發力，與右拳動作同步完成。

圖 42 附圖

(2) Keep the above action, the right foot takes a step rightward into horse stance, at the same time, change the right hand into fist and raise it in front of the right chest with the fist-palm inward, the left fist punches downward, Eyes look rightward. ﹝Figure 42, Attached figure 42﹞

Key points: when punching the fist downward, shake the shoulders to release force, and this action shall be simultaneously completed with that of the right fist.

圖 43

23. 大鵬亮爪
The roc spreads claws

接上勢。身體站立左轉 90°；左腿屈膝上提，重心移至右腿；同時，左拳屈臂後拉，右拳變掌前推，高與肩平，掌心向前，掌指向上；目視前方。（圖 43）

要點：左膝要提高，獨立勢要穩固，推掌要以肩發力，力達掌根。

梅
花
拳
套
路
動
作
圖
解

Follow the above posture, the body stands upright and turns 90° to the left, bend the left knee to raise the leg, shift the barycenter to the right leg. At the same time, bend the left arm to pull the left fist backward, the right fist changes into palm and pushes forward, with the palm forward and fingers up at the shoulders height. Eyes look forward. (Figure 43)

Key points: lift the left knec highly, standing with one foot shall be steady. the shoulder is the force source whe pushing the falm and the force shall reach the end of palm.

圖 44

第三段　Section Three

24. 海底炮
Cannon at the bottom of the sea

(1) 接上勢。左腳向前落步；左手變掌，由前向後畫弧，直臂置於身體左側，掌心向前；同時，右掌變拳，從下向上抬起，掌心向外；提右膝；目視前方。（圖 44）

(1) Follow the above posture, the left foot lands to ground ahead, the left hand changes into palm, draws a curve from front to back, place the left palm at the left side of the body with the arm straight, keep the palm forward. At the same time, the right palm changes into fist and lifts with the fist –center outward, raise the right knee. Eyes look forward. (Figure 44)

圖 45

（2）上動不停。落右腳與左腳併步震腳，雙腿屈膝下蹲；同時，右拳向下砸拳，落於左掌心；目視右拳。（圖 45）

要點：砸拳要沉穩有力，與左掌要有合力。

（2）Keep the above action, fall and stamp with the right foot, and bring it together with the left one, bend the knees to squat. At the same time, the right fist pounds downward and falls to the left palm. Eyes look at the right fist.（Figure 45）

Key points: the fist pounding shall be steady and forceful, and have resultant force with the left palm.

圖 46

25. 馬步架打
Parry and punch in horse stance

（1）接上勢。右腳向右橫跨一步成馬步；右拳前沖，拳心向下，高與肩平；左拳向上擺架於頭頂左上方；目視右方。（圖 46）

（1）Follow the above posture, the right foot strides a step rightward into horse stance; the right fist punches forward with fist-palm down at the shoulders height. The left fist swings upwards and parries above the left part of the head top. Eyes look rightward.（Figure 46）

梅花拳

圖 47

(2) 上動不停。上左腳，同時，以右腳為軸，身體右轉 180°成馬步；右拳向上擺架於頭頂右上方；左拳向前沖出，拳心向下，高與肩平；目視左拳。（圖 47）

要點：馬步架打連續兩次動作，演示時要連貫協調，變換馬步要輕靈、穩健、快捷。

(2) Keep the above action, the left foot steps forward, at the same time, turn the body 180° to the right with the right foot as pivot into horse stance. The right fist swings upward and parries above the right part of the head top, the left fist punches forward with the fist –palm down at the shoulders height. Eyes look at the left fist. (Figure 47)

Key points: performing two successive actions of parry and punch in horse stance shall be coherent and harmonions. changing into horse stance shall be agile, steady and swift.

圖 48

26. 轉身穿喉掌　Turn body thread thorat

(1) 接上勢。身體上提右轉 90°，上左步成左弓步；雙拳收回腰際隨即變掌，掌心向上；重心前移，右掌向前穿出，掌指向前，掌心向上，高與肩平；目視前方。（圖 48）

(1) Follow the above posture, raise the body and turn it to 90° to the right, the left foot steps forward into left bow stance; draw back the two fists to the waist, then change them into palms with the palm up. Shift the baryenter forward, the right palm thread out forward, with the fingers forward and the palm up at the shoulers level. Eyes look forward. ﹝Figure 48﹞

圖 49

(2) 上動不停。右掌收回腰間；左掌隨即向前穿出，掌心向上，掌指向前；目視前方。（圖 49）

要點：兩次穿喉掌要力達掌指，連貫協調。

(2) Keep the above actiion, withdraw the right palm to the waist, then thread the left palm forward with the palm up and fingers forward. Eyes look forward.（Figure 49）

Key points: the forces of threading palms shall reach the fingers, and these two actions shall be completed coherently and harmoniously.

圖 50

27. 後掃腿　Sweeping leg backward

接上勢。身體下蹲，雙手按地，以左腳尖為軸，右腿順時針向後平掃一周；目視右腿。（圖 50）

要點：掃腿要直，力達右腳內側，與雙手緊密配合協調完成。

Follow the above posture, the body squats downward and two hands press the ground. With the left tiptoe as pivot, the right leg horizontally sweeps backward clockwise for a circle. Eyes look at the right leg.〔Figure 50〕

Key points: when sweeping leg backward, the leg shall be straight and the force shall reach the inner side of the right foot, and this action shall be completed harmoniously with the close cooperation of the two hands.

圖 51

28. 連三掌
Linked three palms

(1) 接上勢。起身成右弓步；右掌經腰間向前平推掌，掌心向前；左掌收回腰間；目視右掌。（圖 51）

(1) Follow the above posture, raise the body into right bow stance, the right palm pushes forward horizontally through the waist with the palm forward, withdraw the left palm to the waist. Eyes look at the right palm.（Figure 51）

圖 52

(2) 上動不停。左掌前推；右掌收回於腰間；目視
左掌。（圖 52）

(2) Keep the above action, push the left palm for-ward;
withdraw the right palm to the waist. Eyes look at the left palm.
（Figure 52）

圖 53

(3)上動不停。右掌前推，左掌置於腰際；目視右
掌。（圖 53）

要點：三掌要迅猛連貫，有爆發力，力達掌根。

(3) Keep the above action, push the right plam forward; put
the left palm at the waist. Eyes look at the right palm.（Figure
53）

Key points: the three actions shall be swift and coherent
with explosive force, and the strength shall reach the base of
palm.

圖 54

29. 旋風腳　Whirlwind kick

接上勢。抬左腳，騰空躍起，在空中轉體 360°，同時，空中右腳裏合；左掌拍擊右腳內側。（圖 54）

要點：騰空要高，旋身要疾速，落地要穩當。

Follow the above posture, raise the left foot and jump up, turn the body 360° in the air. At the same time, swing the right foot inward in the air, and the left palm slaps the inner side of the right foot.〔Figure 54〕

Key points: the jump shall be high, body turn shall be swift, and falling to the ground shall be steady.

圖 55

30. 回頭望月
Turn back to look at the moon

（1）接上勢。旋風腳左腳落地，右腳扣左腿膝後；
雙掌在頭頂合擊；目平視前方。（圖 55）

（1）Follow the above posture, the left foot of whirlwind kick
lands to the ground, keep the right foot close to the knee with
toes inward, the two palms claps jointly at the head top. Eyes
look forward horizontally.（Figure 55）

圖 56

　　(2)上動不停。右腳向右落地成橫襠步；左掌向左前方亮掌，掌心向左，掌指向上；右掌在頭頂右上方亮掌，掌心向上，掌指向左；目視左前方。（圖 56）

　　要點：上下動作要連貫流暢，協調完成。

梅花拳套路動作圖解

(2) Keep the above action, the right foot falls to the ground rightward into side bow stance, flash the left palm left forward with palm leftward and fingers up; flash the right palm above the right part of the head top with palm up and fingers leftward. Eyes look left forward. (Figure 56)

Key points: the successive actions shall be coherent and fluent, and completed harmoniously.

圖 57

31. 二起腳
Jumping kick twice

　　接上勢。抬左腳，身體騰空，同時，向左擰腰，右腳向前彈踢；右掌拍擊腳面；目視前方。（圖57）。

　　要點：騰空要擰腰，抖肩發力，力達右腳面，並與右掌要連貫協調，拍擊力點要準確響亮。

梅
花
拳
套
路
動
作
圖
解

Follow the above posture, raise the left foot, the body jumps up. At the same time, the waist twists leftward, the right foot kicks forward, the right palm slaps the instep. Eyes look forward. ﹙Figure 57﹚

Key points: for jumping, twist the waist and snap the shoulders to releasing force that shall reach the right instep, and keep the jump coherent and harmonious with the right palm, pat the instep at an accurate point and with loud sound.

圖 58

32. 白鶴亮翅　White crane spreads wings

(1) 接上勢。身體略右轉，左腳落地成馬步；雙手在胸前交叉，右手在下，左手在上；身體略下蹲，重心移於右腿；目視左手。（圖 58）

(1) Follow the above posture, turn the body rightward slightly, the left foot lands to the ground into horse stance, cross the two hands in front of the chest with the right hand down and the left one up. The body squats slightly, shift the barycenter to the right leg. Eyes look at the left hand.（Figure 58）

圖 59

(2) 上動不停。屈膝上提左腿，重心移於右腿，身體略向左轉；雙掌向兩側平直推出，掌心均向外，掌指均向上，高與肩平；目平視前方。（圖 59）

(2) Keep the above action, bend the knee to raise the left leg, shift the barycenter to the right leg, turn the body leftward slightly. Two palms push horizontally and straight toward both sides of the body, with both of the palms outward and fingers up at the shoulder height. Eyes horizontally look forward. (Figure 59)

圖 60

33. 猿猴束身　The monkey shrinks body

(1) 接上勢。左腳向左前方落步；左掌經胸前向外、向上繞環於體前，掌心向前；右掌向外環繞上提於右肩上方，掌心向前；目視前方。（圖 60）

(1) Follow the above posture, the left foot lands left forward, the left palm circles through the front of the chest outward and upward in front of the body with the palm forward; the right palm circles outward and lifts above the right shoulder with the palm forward. Eyes look forward.（Figure 60）

圖 61

(2)上動不停。收左腳成丁步，身體下蹲，略向左轉；左掌變拳，抱於胸前；右掌下砍於右膝外側；目視右前下方。（圖 61）

(2) Keep the above action, withdraw the left foot into T-stance, the body squats and turns to the left slightly, change the left palm into fist and hold in front of the chest, hack the right palm downward to the outer side of the right knee. Eyes look right downward ahead.（Figure 61）

圖 62

(3) 上動不停。起身，向右前方上右步；右掌向
裏，向外繞環；左掌向後屈肘置於頭部左側；目平視
前方。（圖 62）

(3) Keep the above action, raise the body, the right foot
steps right forward, encircle the right palm inward and outward,
bend the left elbow backward and place the left palm at the left
side of the head. Eyes horizontally look forward. ﹝Figure 62﹞

圖 63

(4) 上動不停。收左腳成丁步；右掌變拳抱於胸前；同時，身體下蹲，向右略轉體；左掌下砍於左膝外側；目視左下方。（圖 63）

要點：砍掌動作要迅猛有力，連貫協調。

(4) Keep the above action, withdraw the left foot into T-stance, change the right palm into fist and hold it in front of the chest. At the same time, the body squats and turns to the right slightly. Hack the left palm downward to the outer side of the left knee. Eyes look left downward. (Figure 63)

Key points: hacking the palm shall be swift and forceful, coherent and harmonious.

圖 64

34. 虎尾腳　Tiger-tail foot

接上勢。左腳抬起向左後方踹腿，重心移於右腿；左掌向左腿方向後推；右拳抱於腰間；目視左腳。（圖 64）

要點：踹腿迅猛有力。

Follow the above posture, raise the left foot and kick sideways left backward, shift the barycenter to the right leg; push the left palm backward toward the left leg, hold the right fist on the waist. Eyes look at the left foot. (Figure 64)

Key points: kicking sideways shall be swift and forceful.

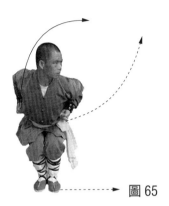

圖 65

35. 猛虎出洞　Fierce tiger goes out of cave

(1)接上勢。左腳向前落地，身體右轉 90°。震右腳併步下蹲；雙掌變拳收回腰間；目視左方。（圖 65）

(1) Follow the above posture, the right foot falls to the ground forward, turn the body 90° to the right. Stamp the right foot, bring the right foot together with the left one and squat. Change the two palms into fists and withdraw them to the waist. Eyes look leftward.（Figure 66）

圖66

（2）上動不停。左腳向前上一步，成左弓步，身體左傾；雙拳向左上方沖出，肘微屈，拳心相對；目視左方。（圖66）

要點：沖拳要抖肩發力，力達拳面。

梅
花
拳
套
路
動
作
圖
解

(2) Keep the above action, the left foot takes a step forward into left bow stance, slant the body leftward; punch the two fists left upward. Slightly bend the elbow with the palm sides opposite. Eyes look leftward. (Figure 66)

Key points: when striking the fists, snap the shoulder to exert strength that shall reach the fist–face.

圖 67

第四段　Section Four

36. 墊步拐肘　Elbow bending with skip step

接上勢。震右腳，上左腳成弓步；右拳回收，屈臂向左前方斜擊肘；左掌同時回抱拍擊右前臂；目視前方。（圖 67）

要點：擊肘要抖肩發力，力達右肘外側。

梅
花
拳
套
路
動
作
圖
解

Follow the above posture, stamp with the right foot, the left foot steps forward into bow stance. Withdraw the right fist and bend the arm to strike the elbow left forward aslant, at the same time, the left palm holds back and claps the right forearm. Eyes look forward. ﹝ Figure 67 ﹞

Key points: for elbow striking, snap the shoulders to release force that shall reach the outer side of the right elbow.

圖 68

37. 轉身反背拳
Backhand fist with body turn

接上勢。身體右轉 180°成右弓步；右拳從懷中向前翻臂擊打，拳心向內，拳眼向右；左拳附於右肘下方；目平視右拳。（圖 68）

要點：轉身要輕靈，反背拳要迅猛，力達拳背。

Follow the above posture, turn the body 180° to the right into right bow stance, the right fist strikes forward through turning over the arm from bosom, keep the fist –palm inward, the fist–hole rightward, and the left fist close to the lower part of the right elbow. Eyes look at the right fist horizontally. ﹙Figure 68﹚

Key points: turn the body agilely, backhand fist shall be quick and forceful with the force reaching the back of the fist.

圖 69

38. 撤步打三拳
Step back and punch three times

（1）接上勢。身體左轉 180°，退左步；左手掄架於頭頂左方；右拳前沖，與肩同高，拳面向前；目平視右拳。（圖 69）

(1) Follow the above posture, turn the body180° to the left, withdraw the left foot, swing and parry the left hand above the left part of head top, the right fist strikes forward at the shoulders height, with the fist –plane forward. Eyes look at the right fist horizontally.（Figure 69）

圖 70

(2) 上動不停。身體右轉 180°，退右步，右拳掄架於頭頂右上方，左拳前沖，拳面向前；目視左方。（圖 70）

(2) Keep the above action, turn the body180° to the right, withdraw the right foot, swing and parry with the right fist above the right part of head top, the left fist strikes forward with fist-plane forward, Eyes look leftward. (Figure 70)

圖 71

（3）上動不停。身體左轉 180°，退左腳成馬步；左
拳掄架於頭頂左上方；右拳前沖，高與肩平，拳面向
前；目視右拳。（圖 71）

要點：撤步、轉身與沖拳連續三次動作要連貫協
調，迅捷靈活。

(3)Keep the above action, turn the body 180° to the left, withdraw the left foot into horse stance, swing and parry the left fist above the left part of head top. The right fist strikes forward at the shoulders level, with fist–plane forward. Eyes look at the right fist. (Figure 71)

Key points: stepping backward, turning the body and striking the fist, these three continual actions shall be coherent and harmonious, swift and agile.

圖 72

39. 馬步單鞭
Single whip in horse stance

接上勢。以右腳為軸，上左腳，身體右轉 180°成馬步；兩拳變掌，經胸前交叉，向兩側水平推出，掌心向外，掌指向上，臂與肩平；目視左掌。（圖 72）

要點：推掌要勁力迅猛。

梅
花
拳
套
路
動
作
圖
解

Follow the above posture, the left foot steps forward and turn the body180° to the right with the right foot as pivot into horse stance. Change the two fists into palms, and cross them through the front of the chest, then push them horizontally to both sides of the body, with the palm outward and the fingers up, keep the arms at the shoulders height. Eyes look at the left palm. (Figure 72)

Key point: pushing the palm shall be swift and forceful.

圖73

40. 臥地炮 Ground cannon

接上勢。身體右轉 90°，上右腳，震腳併步；同時，左手翻腕變拳，抱於胸前，拳心向裏；身體下蹲，右掌變拳下栽；目視右拳。（圖 73）

要點：栽拳要抖肩發力，力達拳面。

Follow the above posture, turn the body 90° to the right, the right foot steps forward, stamp and bring feet together. At the same time, the left hand turns over the wrist into fist and holds in front of the chest with fist –palm of the fist inward, the body squats, change the right palm into fist and punch it downward. Eyes look at the right fist.〔Figure 73〕

Key points: when punching the fist downward, snap the shoulders to release force that shall reach the fist–plane.

圖74

41. 沖天炮　Sky cannon

接上勢。起身直立；左手在胸前摟抓變拳；震右
腳；右拳從左拳內側向上方屈肘沖出，隨即回收，拳
心向內；目視前方。（圖74）

要點：沖拳要有反彈力。

Follow the above posture, the body stands up, the left hand
grabs in front of the chest and changes into fist, stamp the right
foot, bend the right elbow and strike upward from the inner side
of the left one, then draw it back with the fist – palm inward.
Eyes look forward.（Figure 74）

Key point: thrust the fist with rebound force.

圖 75

42. 臥枕
Rest on the pillow

接上勢。左腳向左撤出一步成左弓步，上體左傾；左拳屈肘回抱於左胸前；右拳向前下栽，拳面向下，拳心向裏；目視右方。（圖 75、圖 75 附圖）

圖 75 附圖

Follow the above posture, withdraw the left foot a step leftward into left bow stance, slant the upper body to the left, bend the left elbow and hold the left fist back to the front of the left chest, the right fist punches down forward with fist-plane down and fist-palm inward. Eyes look rightward, (Figure 75, Attached figure 75)

圖 76

43. 地蹚掃腿　Sweep leg on the ground

（1）接上勢。雙手按地；左腿屈膝，左腳尖點地，右腿向前、向左橫掃；目視右腳。（圖 76）

（1）Follow the above posture, press two hands on the ground, bend the knee of the left leg with left tiptoe on the floor, the right leg sweeps horizontally forward and leftward. Eyes look at the right foot.〔Figure 76〕

圖 77

(2)上動不停。左腳離地讓右腿橫掃一周，左腳落地成右仆步姿勢；目視右腳。（圖 77）

要點：掃腿要伸直，力達腳面內側，並與雙手緊密配合。

(2) Keep the above action, the left foot leaves ground to let the right leg sweep horizontally for a circle, the left foot lands to the ground into right crouch stance. Eyes look at the right foot. (Figure 77)

Key points: when sweeping leg, unbend the leg with strength reaching the inner side of instep, and the close cooperation of two hands.

圖 78

44. 丁步亮掌　Flash palm in T-stance

（1）接上勢。身體站立；左腳向右撤半步；雙掌向左掄擺；目視左方。（圖 78）

(1) Follow the above posture, the body stands up. Withdraw the left foot a half-step rightward; swing the two palms to the left. Eyes look leftward.〔Figure 78〕

圖 79

　　⑵上動不停。左腳收回成丁步；同時，身體下蹲；雙掌經胸前向右前方推出，右臂與肩同高，掌心向前，掌指向上；左掌屈肘亮掌於胸前，掌心向右，掌指向上；目視右掌。（圖 79）

　　⑵ Keep the above action, the left foot draws back into T-stance. At the same time, the body squats, and the two palms push left forward through the front of chest. Keep the right arm at the shoulders level with the palm forward and fingers up; bend the left elbow and flash the left palm in front of the chest, with the palm rightward and fingers up. Eyes look at the right palm. （Figure 79）

圖 80

45. 猛虎跳澗　Fierce tiger jumps over gully

⑴ 接上勢。起身，左腳向左上步；雙掌在頭上方合擊；目平視左前方。（圖 80）

⑴ Follow the above posture, raise the body, the left foot takes a step leftward, the two palms clap over the head. Eyes look left forward horizontally.（Figure 80）

圖 81

(2)上動不停。兩腳蹬地躍起；同時，右掌變拳抱於右腰間；左掌立於右胸前，掌心向右；目視左方。（圖 81）

(2) Keep the above action, the two feet press against ground and jump up. At the same time, change the right palm into fist and hold on the right waist, stand the left palm in front of the right chest with palm rightward. Eyes look leftward.（Figure 81）

圖 82

（3）上動不停。雙腳落地成左仆步；左掌向左腳方向切掌；目視左腳。（圖82）

要點：騰空要高，仆步、切掌動作要快捷連貫，同時完成。

(3) Keep the above action, the two feet land to the ground into left crouch stance, cut with the left palm toward the left foot. Eyes look at the left foot. 〔 Figure 82 〕

Key points: jump up highly, changing into crouch stance and cutting the palm shall be quick and coherent, simultane – ously completed.

圖 83

46. 馬步沖拳　Thrust fist in horse stance

接上勢。身體左轉 180°，上右腳成馬步；同時，左掌向前摟抓變拳，收回腰間；右拳向右平沖，拳心向下，與肩同高；目視右拳。（圖 83）。

要點：沖拳要抖肩發力，力達拳面。

Follow the above posture, turn the body 180° to the left, the right foot steps forward into horse stance, at the same time, grab the left hand forward into fist, and draw it back on the waist. The right fist strikes rightward horizontally with the fist–palm down at the shoulders height. Eyes look at the right fist.（Figure 83）

Key points: when striking forward, snap the shoulders to exert strength that shall reach the fist–plane.

圖 84

47. 舞花坐山　Swing arms with horse stance

（1）接上勢。起身，震右腳；左腳扣於右腿膕窩處；右臂向後、向下掄；左拳屈肘擺架於頭頂左上方；目視右後側。（圖 84）

（1）Follow the above posture, raise the body and stamp with the right foot, keep the left foot close to the right hamstring The right arm swings backward and downward, bend the left elbow, parry and place the left fist over the head. Eyes look right backward.（Figure 84）

梅花拳套路動作圖解

圖 85

(2) 上動不停。左腳向左落步成馬步；左拳按於左膝上，身體下蹲；右拳擺架於頭頂，拳心向前上方；目視左方。（圖 85）

要點：擰腰靈活不僵，上下動作協調一致。

(2) Keep the above action, land the left foot leftward into horse stance, press the left fist on the left knee, squat the body, swing and place the right fist over the head top, with fist–palm upward ahead. Eyes look leftward. (Figure 85)

Key points: twist the waist agilely, and the actions shall be harmonious and coherent.

圖 86

48. 收勢　Closing form

（1）接上勢。左腳回收併步；雙拳抱於腰間；目視前方。（圖 86）

(1) Follow the above posture, draw left foot back and bring feet together, and hold the two palms on the waist. Eyes look forward.（Figure 86）

圖 87

　(2) 上動不停。雙手自然下垂成立正式；目視前方。（圖 87）

　要點：平心靜氣，體態自然，精神內斂。

　(2) Keep the above action, two hands drop naturally, and stand at attention. Eyes look forward. (Figure 87)

　Key points: be calm in natural posture, and collect the vital energy inward.

梅花拳

全套動作演示圖

Demonstration of All the Action

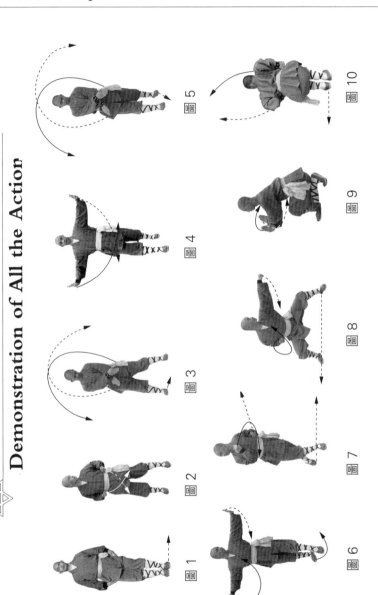

圖 1　圖 2　圖 3　圖 4　圖 5

圖 6　圖 7　圖 8　圖 9　圖 10

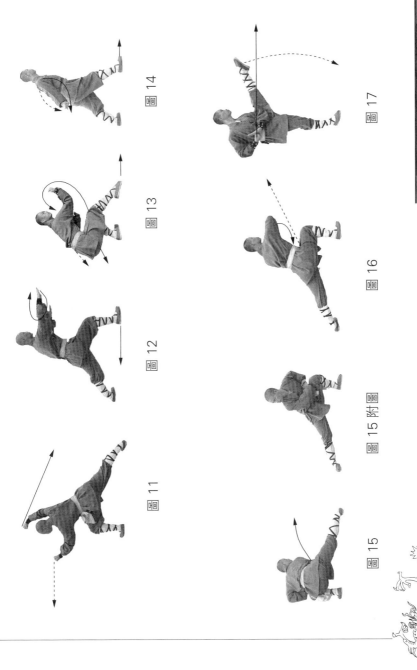

全套動作示意圖

梅
花
拳

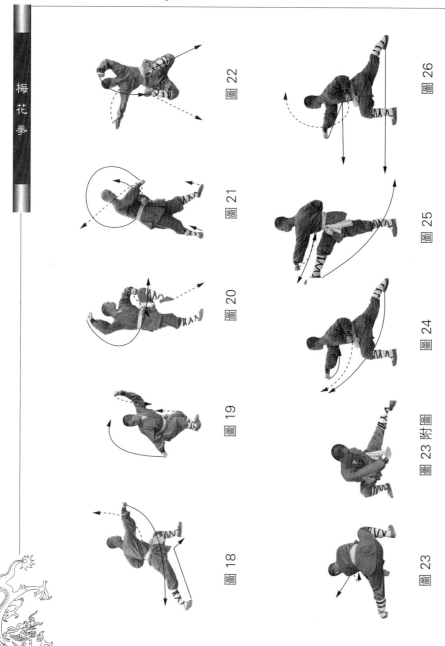

圖 22

圖 21

圖 20

圖 19

圖 18

圖 26

圖 25

圖 24

圖 23 附圖

圖 23

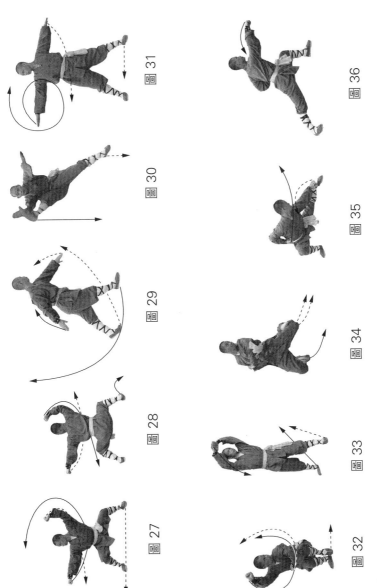

全套動作示意圖

梅花拳

圖 41

圖 40

圖 39

圖 38

圖 37

圖 45

圖 44

圖 43

圖 42 附圖

圖 42

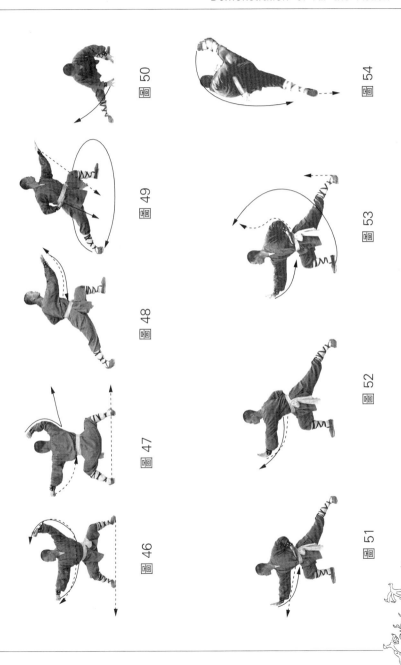

圖 50

圖 54

圖 49

圖 53

圖 48

圖 52

圖 47

圖 51

圖 46

全套動作示意圖

梅
花
拳

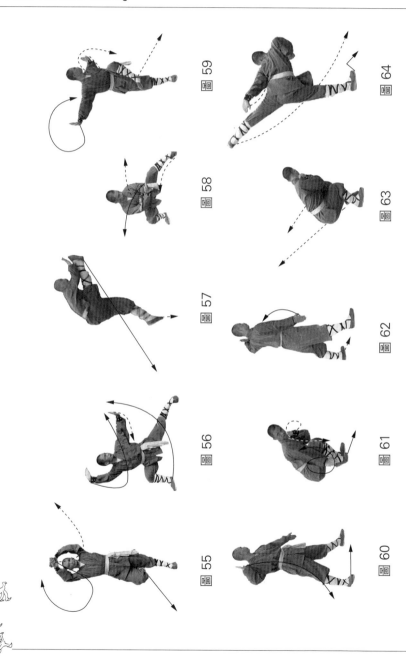

圖 59

圖 58

圖 57

圖 56

圖 55

圖 64

圖 63

圖 62

圖 61

圖 60

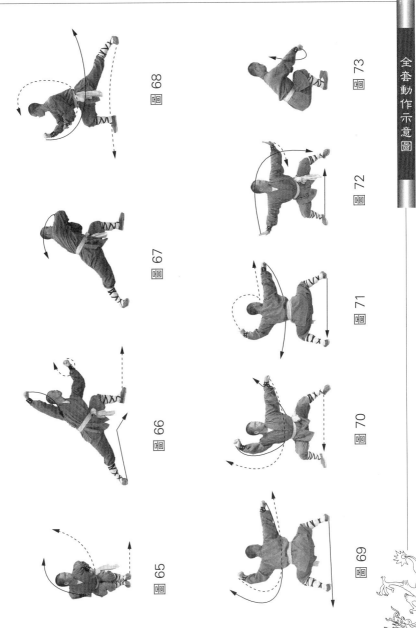

全套動作示意圖

圖 68

圖 67

圖 66

圖 65

圖 73

圖 72

圖 71

圖 70

圖 69

梅花拳

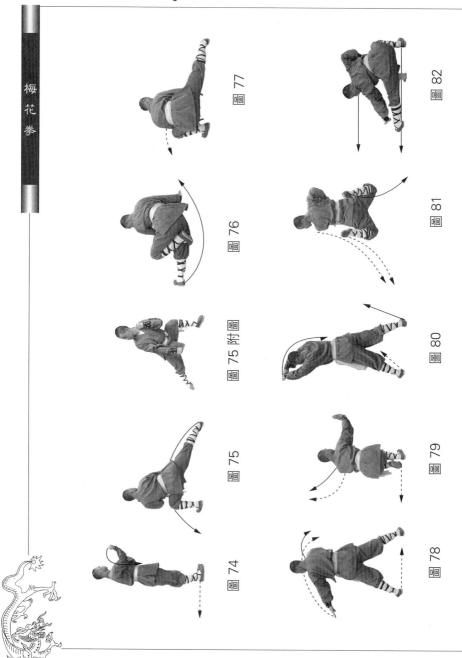

圖 77

圖 76

圖 75 附

圖 75

圖 74

圖 82

圖 81

圖 80

圖 79

圖 78

图 87

图 86

图 85

图 84

图 83

全套動作示意圖

導引養生功 系列叢書

張廣德養生著作

每冊定價 350 元

全系列為彩色圖解附教學光碟

彩色圖解太極武術

1 太極功夫扇

定價220元

2 武當太極劍

定價220元

3 楊式太極劍

定價220元

4 楊式太極刀

定價220元

5 二十四式太極拳＋VCD

定價350元

6 三十二式太極劍＋VCD

定價350元

7 四十二式太極劍＋VCD

定價350元

8 四十二式太極拳＋VCD

定價350元

9 楊式十六式太極劍拳

定價350元

10 楊氏二十八式太極拳＋VCD

定價350元

11 楊式太極拳四十式＋VCD

定價350元

12 陳式太極拳五十六式＋VCD

定價350元

13 吳式太極拳五十六式＋VCD

定價350元

14 精簡陳式太極拳八式十六式

定價220元

15 精簡吳式太極拳架‧推手三十六式

定價220元

16 夕陽美功夫扇

定價220元

17 綜合四十八式太極拳＋VCD

定價350元

18 三十二式太極拳 四段

定價220元

19 楊式三十七式太極拳＋VCD

定價350元

20 楊氏五十一式太極劍＋VCD

定價350元

國家圖書館出版品預行編目資料

梅花拳＝Plum-blossom Boxing／耿 軍 著
——初版，——臺北市，大展，2007〔民96〕
面；21公分，——（少林傳統功夫漢英對照系列；7）
ISBN 978-957-468-563-9（平裝）
1.拳術—中國
528.97 96015113

梅 花 拳

ISBN 978-957-468-563-9

著　　者／耿　軍
責任編輯／孔 令 良
發 行 人／蔡 森 明
出 版 者／大展出版社有限公司
社　　址／台北市北投區（石牌）致遠一路2段12巷1號
電　　話／（02）28236031·28236033·28233123
傳　　眞／（02）28272069
郵政劃撥／01669551
網　　址／www.dah-jaan.com.tw
E-mail／service@dah-jaan.com.tw
登 記 證／局版臺業字第2171號
承 印 者／傳興印刷有限公司
裝　　訂／建鑫裝訂有限公司
排 版 者／弘益電腦排版有限公司
授 權 者／北京人民體育出版社
初版1刷／2007年（民96年）10月

定　價／180元

大展好書　好書大展
品嚐好書　冠群可期

大展好書　好書大展
品嘗好書　冠群可期